PULLMAN

JoAnne McFarland

GRID BOOKS · BOSTON

GRID BOOKS
grid-books.org

The section *Pathfinder* first appears as *Pullman, a meditation on loss* in the digital collection *Tracks of My Tears*, published online by The Word Works in 2020.

Cover: The Pathfinder Dress, 2022

Dress images included in *Pullman* are part of an ongoing collage series begun by the author in 1997.
In order of appearance:

The Lovin' Spoonful Dress
The Golden Goose Dress
The Note to Self Dress
The Prim Rose Dress
The Bending the Horizon Line Dress
The Mouthing Off Dress
My Imaginary Boo Dress
The Monster of Power Dress
The Force of Nature Dress
The Endangered Species Dress
The Monarch Dress

ISBN 978-1-946830-16-6
First Edition

For my parents

John and Glo

The Pullman Car Company operated railroad cars, including sleepers, during the late 19th Century through much of the 20th Century. Most of the porters on the trains were African-American men. Thousands belonged to The Brotherhood of Sleeping Car Porters, founded and organized by A. Philip Randolph. It became one of the most influential labor unions of the 20th Century.

SLEEPER

Don't break into this poem.

Please, just let it be.

Let it arrange itself without your intervention.

And if it be too neat, sit by it, and breathe.

Breathe as evenly as it breathes.

Break into this poem and it will not vanish.

It will merely sink.

Just last night, my daughter Misha told me that humiliate

means to sink down into the earth.

A poem can die like that. I worry about

her. Then I remind myself

worry is a kind of invasion, a lack of faith,

a sort of mucking. And after all, didn't she arrive

right when I most needed love?

Don't break into this poem.

Don't workshop it. Don't nick it with your history.

Everything that has brought you to this point is

your poem.

I crouched in weeds in a vacant lot

on Rosedale Avenue when I was a girl,

in a wild part of The Bronx, past the dead end sign,

before I knew what a metaphor was.

Metaphors have not

improved my life. I understand they may have

improved yours. One day, we might gather around an oak table

in an academic setting and debate the value of symbols.

In dream after dream I crouch, giddy from not

searching, from knowing I am not missing.

Don't change this poem.

I'm trying to save somebody's life.

This is how *I* do it.

True, I'm using a tool few believe in.

Where I come from, lack of belief is a sport,

bitterness a performance, irony a style.

I know an exquisite young woman who cries herself to sleep.

She should be as unhappy as she seems.

She's right—so much of the world has been ruined.

She takes words apart for sport,

then arranges them so they build like an orgasm.

Please don't tell me how to write this.

Don't show me the extra word in line 1,

or how my use of the word "is" drags the whole poem down,

evidence of my lack of proper schooling.

Why doesn't anyone talk about this need to have beauty

proved?

I don't have to prove the worth of my words.

Meaning, if this poem is written (because I write it)

and no one reads it,

it still has value.

Please don't get a group together to discuss whether

this poem is "working."

It's working.

I started writing this poem in 1988, when my father

knocked out my mother, and we both shook with the blows.

All I was doing was listening. He dragged himself into the

distance while I remained fastened to her,

keeping her from becoming a ghost.

I'm writing this for all that I've lost.

Honoring my life this way is inexpensive.

It's refusing to grieve that has cost me.

My refusal to grieve broke a man I loved.

He wept for me, even as I refused to weep.

I thought I could get away with it—

my lustrous, grief-less life.

I had a lot of support.

Now, grief fills my pages.

Every poem I write is a lullaby.

Oncc upon a time there were men who helped other

men reach their destinations.

They carried their coats and cases, served them their

meals and liquor, then tucked them up in their beds.

This poem prepares you to let your guard down,

that's its job.

It treats you like a child.

They treated them like children

It's a mistake to assume life moves from point A to point B,

that the future will come after whatever this is,

and that some are born to be carriers, while others are meant

to be praised.

PATHFINDER

Background text: *Incidents in the Life of a Slave Girl* by Harriet Jacobs, first published in 1861

STATION

I have promised to tell you the truth, and
I will do it honestly, let it cost me what it

Flames

may. I will not try to screen myself behind
the plea of compulsion from a master, for it
was not so. Neither can I plead ignorance or
thoughtlessness. For years, my master had
done his utmost to pollute my mind with
foul images, and to destroy the pure princi-

scour the

ples inculcated by my grandmother, and the
good mistress of my childhood. The influ-
ences of slavery had had the same effect on
me that they had on other young girls. They
had made me prematurely knowing, con-
cerning the evil ways of the world. I knew
what I did, and I did it with deliberate cal-

mindscape

culation. But, O, ye happy women, whose
purity has been sheltered from childhood,
who have been free to choose the objects of

your affection, whose homes are protected by law, do not judge the poor desolate slave girl too severely! If slavery had been abolished, I, also, could have married the man of my choice. I could have had a home shielded by the laws, and I should have been spared the painful task of confessing what I am now about to relate, but all my prospects had been blighted by slavery. I wanted to keep myself pure, and, under the most adverse circumstances, I tried to preserve my self-respect, but I was struggling alone in the powerful grasp of the demon Slavery, and the monster proved too strong for me. I felt as if I were forsaken by God and man, as if all my efforts must be frustrated, and I became reckless in my despair. It chanced that a white unmarried gentleman had obtained

My vow

was built

of

paper

some knowledge of the circumstances in which I was placed. He knew my grand-

Your love

mother, and often spoke to me in the street. He became interested in me, and asked questions about my master, which I answered in part. He expressed a great deal of sympathy, and a wish to aid me. He constantly sought opportunities to see me, and wrote to me fre-

held no

quently. I was a poor slave girl, only fifteen years old. So much attention from a superior was, of course, flattering, for human nature is the same in all. I also felt grateful for his sympathy, and encouraged by his kind words. It seemed to me a great thing to have such a friend. By degrees, a more tender feeling crept into my heart. He was an educated and eloquent gentleman, too eloquent, alas,

scent

for the poor slave girl who trusted him. Of

course I saw whither all this was tending. To be an object of interest to a man who is not married, and who is not her master, is agreeable to the pride and feelings of a slave, if her miserable situation has left her any pride or sentiment. It seems less degrading to give one's self than to submit to compulsion. There is something akin to freedom in having a lover who has no control over you, except that which he gains by kindness and attachment. A master may treat you as rudely as he pleases, and you dare not speak. The condition of a slave confuses all principles of morality, and, in fact, renders the practice of them impossible. I knew nothing would enrage my master so much as to know that I favored another, and it was something to triumph over my tyrant even in that small

Once upon a time

there was

we

way. I thought he would revenge himself by selling me, and I was sure my friend would buy me. He was a man of more generosity and feeling than my master, and I thought my freedom could be easily obtained from him. The crisis of my fate now came so near that I was desperate. I shuddered to think of being the mother of children that should be owned by my old tyrant. Of a man who was not my master I could ask to have my children well supported, and in this case, I felt confident I should obtain the boon. I also felt quite sure that they would be made free. With all these thoughts revolving in my mind, and seeing no other way of escaping the doom I so much dreaded, I made a headlong plunge. Pity me, and pardon me, O virtuous reader! You never knew what it is to be

Now

I

spill the reasons

a slave, to be entirely unprotected by law or custom, to have the laws reduce you to the condition of a chattel, entirely subject to the will of another. You never exhausted your ingenuity in avoiding the snares, and eluding the power of a hated tyrant, you never shuddered at the sound of his footsteps, and trembled within hearing of his voice. I know I did wrong. No one can feel it more sensibly than I do. The painful and humiliating memory will haunt me to my dying day. Still, in looking back, calmly, on the events of my life, I feel that the slave woman ought not to be judged by the same standard as others. I write only that whereof I know. I was twenty-one years in that cage of obscene birds. I can testify, from my own experience and observation, that slavery is a curse to

Our sure thing

divided into

pleas

the whites as well as to the blacks. It makes white fathers cruel and sensual, the sons violent and licentious. It contaminates the daughters, and makes the wives wretched. And as for the colored race, it needs an abler pen than mine to describe the extremity of their sufferings, the depth of their degradation. If you want to be fully convinced of the abominations of slavery, go on a southern plantation, and call yourself a negro trader. Then there will be no concealment, and you will see and hear things that will seem to you impossible among human beings with immortal souls. When my babe was born, they said it was premature. It weighed only four pounds, but God let it live. I heard the doctor say I could not survive till morning. I had often prayed for death, but now I did

because

I wouldn't be

fetched

not want to die, unless my child could die too. Many weeks passed before I was able

calmed or

to leave my bed. I was a mere wreck of my former self. For a year there was scarcely a day when I was free from chills and fever. My babe was also sickly. His little limbs were often racked with pain. Dr. Flint continued his visits, to look after my health, and he did not fail to remind me that my child was an addition to his stock of slaves. As the months passed, my boy improved in health. When he was a year old, they called him beautiful. The little vine was taking deep root in my existence, though its clinging fondness excited a mixture of love and pain. When I was

cleaned

most sorely oppressed I found solace in his smiles. I loved to watch his infant slumbers, but always there was a dark cloud over my

Now I'm buried

in

your

keening

enjoyment. I could never forget that he was a slave. Sometimes I wished that he might die in infancy. God tried me. My darling became very ill. The bright eyes grew dull, and the little feet and hands were so icy dull that I thought death had already touched them. I had prayed for his death, but never so earnestly as I now prayed for his life, and my prayer was heard. Alas, what mockery it is for a slave mother to try to pray back her dying child to life! Death is better than slavery. It was a sad thought that I had no name to give my child. His father caressed him and treated him kindly, whenever he had a chance to see him. He was not unwilling that he should bear his name, but he had no legal claim to it, and if I had bestowed it upon him, my master would have regarded it as a new

crime, a new piece of insolence, and would, perhaps, revenge it on the boy. O, the serpent of Slavery has many poisonous fangs! Why does the slave ever love? Why allow the tendrils of the heart to twine around ob-

the gasps you

jects which may at any moment be wrenched away by the hand of violence? When separations come by the hand of death, the pious soul can bow in resignation, and say, "Not my will, but thine be done, O Lord!" But when the ruthless hand of man strikes the blow, regardless of the misery he causes, it is

cast

hard to be submissive. I did not reason thus when I was a young girl. Youth will be youth. I loved and I indulged the hope that the dark clouds around me would turn out a bright lining. I forgot that in the land of my birth the shadows are too dense for light to penetrate.

STATION

TRACKS

At me you refuse to look

stare at the past

I'm holding blue I collapse around

No sky in the future Piece me to the front

Imagine honor dancing in filth

gaze Gaze

Here	touch
I lean to see	no
meaning	anywhere
I fear not	killing
intruders	blasts
	Enter
crawl inside me	universe

A bowl is not   a path

unblessed   thirst

drought   separates

rain drops   lust

seeds   from the sea

Now it's woods

Snows

not grief   This heaven

something always   borning

falls forward   blows tumble

resolve   becomes

bubbles

free   tenses

Where

immaterial are you

death's dream Remember

to bury the grains shiver

collect from the bottom

cell souls the soul's cells

and keep on fire

Steam	Pour
porcelain cups	the way out
water has a memory	frozen
wash	soldiers on the lines
your fortune	notes
cadence	
folly	from pistons

Cloud	gray milk
blackbird	white rose
no trouble	yesterday
blood red	lace collars
Yes ma'am	lily
ticket	starched
license	

Smoke columns

newsprint and coffee cream wrist

weeds bed

unfinished whistling

this time city

Pull man

LABOR

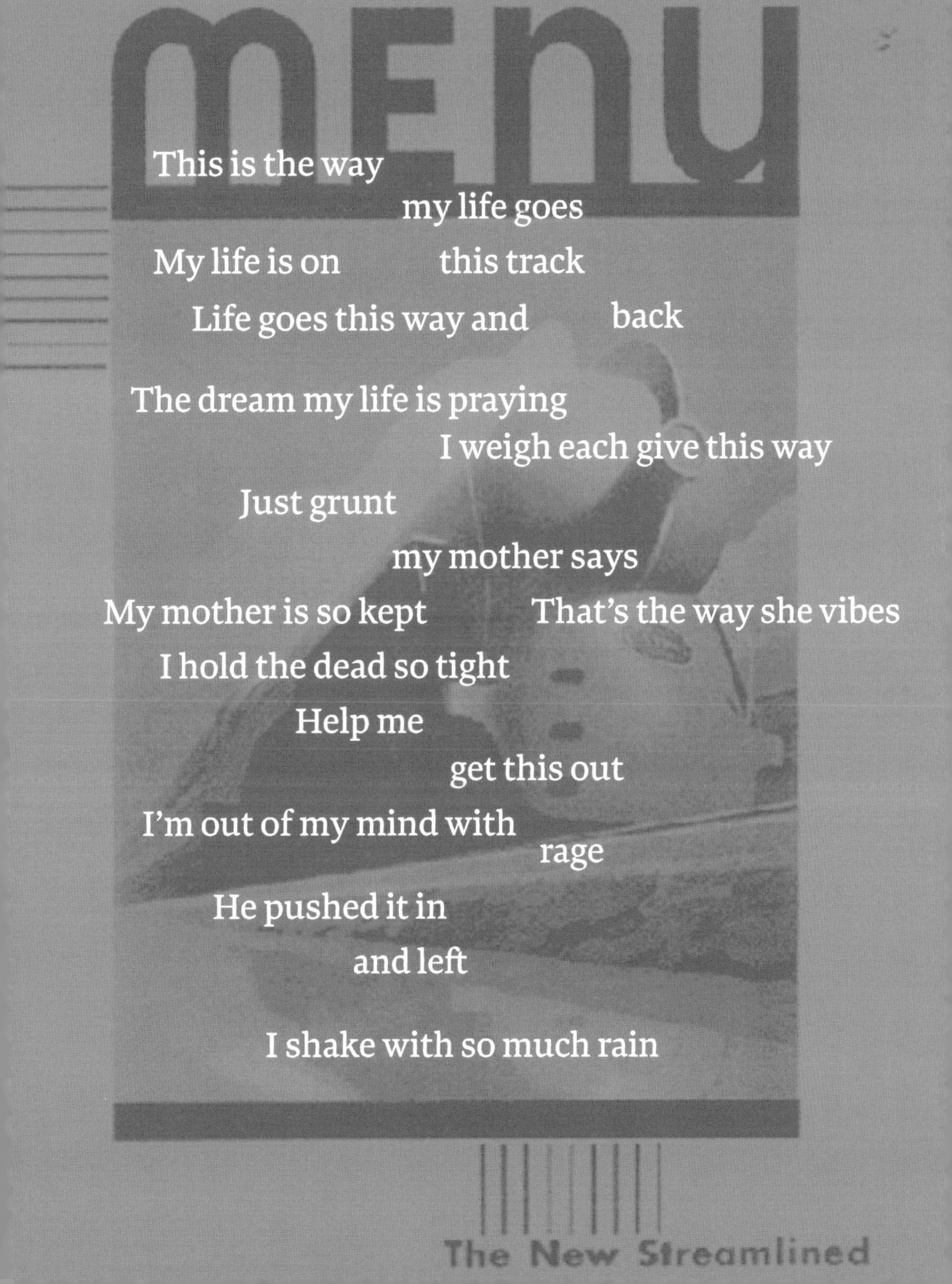

This is the way
my life goes
My life is on this track
Life goes this way and back

The dream my life is praying
I weigh each give this way
Just grunt
my mother says
My mother is so kept That's the way she vibes
I hold the dead so tight
Help me
get this out
I'm out of my mind with
rage
He pushed it in
and left

I shake with so much rain

My insides are so slick

Something grabs my feet

There is no room

for lift

Who will heft this lead

I left my face in the dark

every move it makes

All night I feel it creep

every bit of me resists

How fleet I used to seem

Moves I made to flee

So quick a feather

I pretend to like her
gasps

I leave skid marks
on the table
Its roar lifts my haunches
this lick that lap
so rank
My insides steeped in hisses
It has a pretty heart
she chimes

She pins the scan
to my map
I wipe myself

and dress
I leave my ghost

on the liner

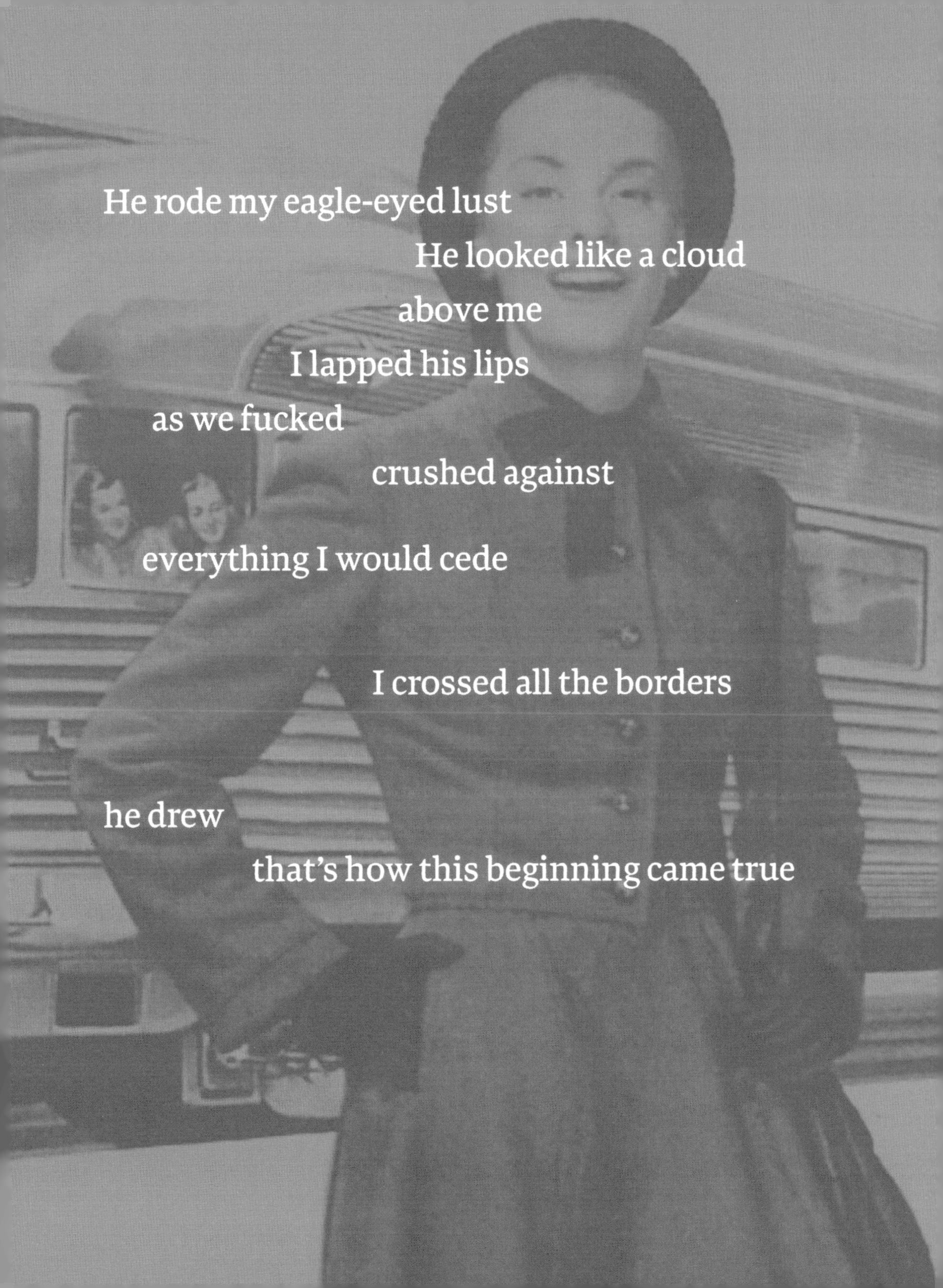

He rode my eagle-eyed lust
He looked like a cloud
above me
I lapped his lips
as we fucked
crushed against
everything I would cede

I crossed all the borders

he drew
that's how this beginning came true

ROUTES & FLOWERS

ROSE

I’ve quit asking why he

has five petals

loses track of me in the dark

The moans I make confuse us both

He can’t follow my plea

used as a symbol

I am spinning

Look at me go

How he roughs up my slit

commonly called “thorn”

If only he trusted me

the scent might bloom

LILY

I'll never know how he feels

when he enters
deep in the ground

I look into his eyes

I see how this world might end

My territory
includes spots and brushstrokes

shifts and swells
a basal rosette of leaves

not giving him a scintilla of

reason

JASMINE

He compares me to the nearest

symbol of divine hope

beautiful thing

I shimmer in the center of the mirror

The room dissolves

He removes his elbow from the glass

exquisite against the dark green

the silvery vortex of everything we own

I dream the vomit away

renowned for its intense fragrance

There are no seasons to waste

HYACINTH

I arrange myself against the wall
providing contrast

An open window to the east

There is nothing more to

free
they do not need room

No one left to call

My face could be
toxic

a lyric

IRIS

In trouble
foliage intact

I speed past the gate

I nail him fast

then watch the world unravel
shaped like a fan

Down and down he drills

Where does hell stop?

Where do the worst days burn?

How will I become
the Greek goddess of the rainbow

holy again?

VIOLET

I have a nasty streak

since at least 500 B.C.

I moved here

from the South

Everything is a cistern or a sewer

every man a fool or

four petals pointing upwards

a sap

I don’t do well with tides

TULIP

He will leave a scar

unfolding stars

I feel him swell

He backs me into his fingers

I drench him with my

highly symmetrical

theme

Is this floor real

Or are we humping

in damp nutritionally rich soil

a cloud?

AMARYLLIS

Everything gravitates to use

From the bed I can smell the melon rinds

in the sink

My ankles clasp his cheeks
out of direct sunlight

Late morning I think
a deep burgundy

No one cares

who spilled the honey

GARDENIA

He first-persons my lust
creamiest white

No doubt I could be shot or stoned
move to a sheltered location

The way in resembles the way out

once you cede a need for direction

It has cost me

I live on kisses for a week
reflecting the moonlight

a single night for one hundred days

WHISTLES & STOPS

Lyrics: John L. McFarland
Art: JoAnne McFarland
Facts: The Negro Almanac of 1972

WON'T BE LONG

Here I am
By the railroad track
Waiting for my baby
He's coming back

Coming back to me
On the 503
And I won't be long
No, I won't be long

I get so lonesome
Since the man has been gone
There ain't a thing worth mentioning
Nothing been going on

And that's why I know
When the whistle blows
Yeah, that I won't be long
No, no, I won't be long

My daddy told me
When he said goodbye, yes, he did
"I'll be back, baby
Baby, bye and bye"

And that's why I waited
So doggone long, yeah
Can't you see how happy I am?
Because the man is coming home

So now, here I be
By the railroad track
Oh, waiting for my baby
He's coming back

Coming back to me
On the 503
Yeah, and I won't be long
No, no, I won't be long

I ain't had no loving
Since you know when
He's a long gone rooster
And I'm a lonesome hen

And that's why I'm sure
When the whistle blows
Yeah, that I won't be long
No, no, I won't be long
I'm so excited
My knees are shaking, yeah
Mr. Engineer
Don't you keep me waiting

Hear me telling you
Hurry, hurry, hurry, hurry
Hurry, hurry, hurry, hurry
Baby, here I am
Oh, by the railroad track
Waiting for my baby
He's coming back

Coming back to me
Lord, on the 503
Yeah and I won't be long

No, I won't be long

Yeah, I know
When the whistle blows
Hey, I won't be long
No, no, I won't be long

DEPEW

1704

Elias Neau, a Frenchman, opens a school for Negro slaves.

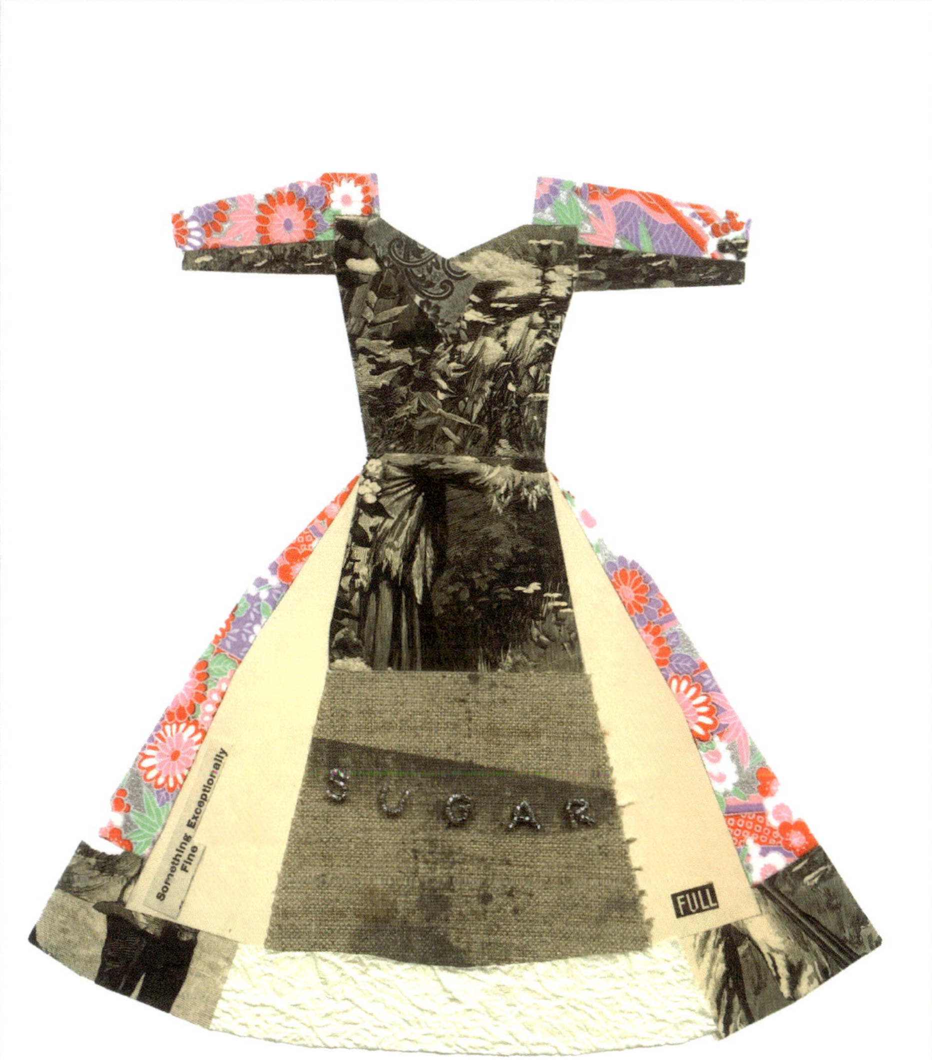

SUGAR
Something Exceptionally Fine
FULL

KEWANEE

1870

Joseph H. Rainey is seated as the first Negro in the House of Representatives.

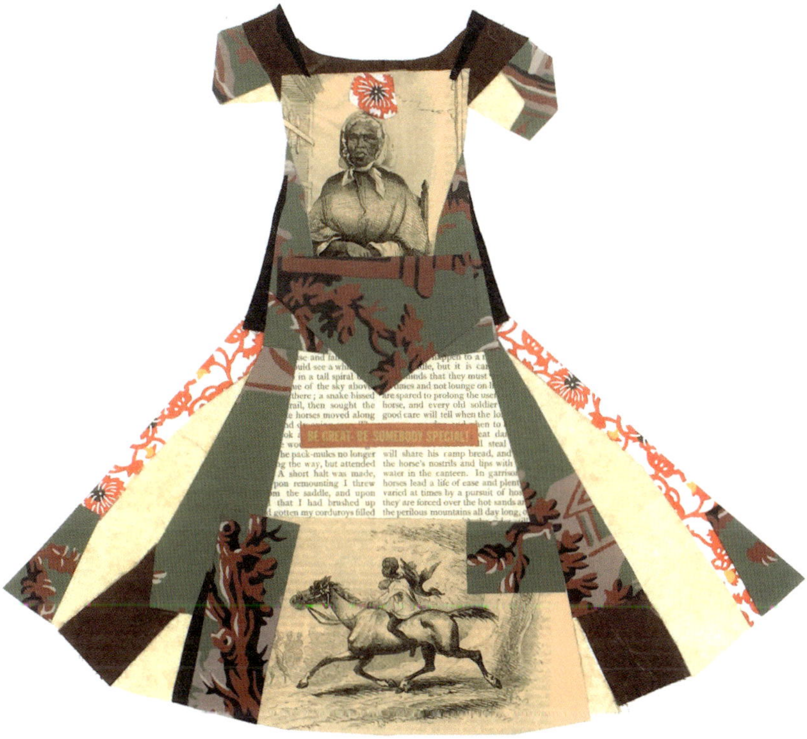
BE GREAT. BE SOMEBODY SPECIAL!

RED WING

1888

Founding of two Negro banks—The Savings Bank of the Grand Fountain United Order of True Reformers in Virginia, and the Capital Savings Bank in Washington, D.C.

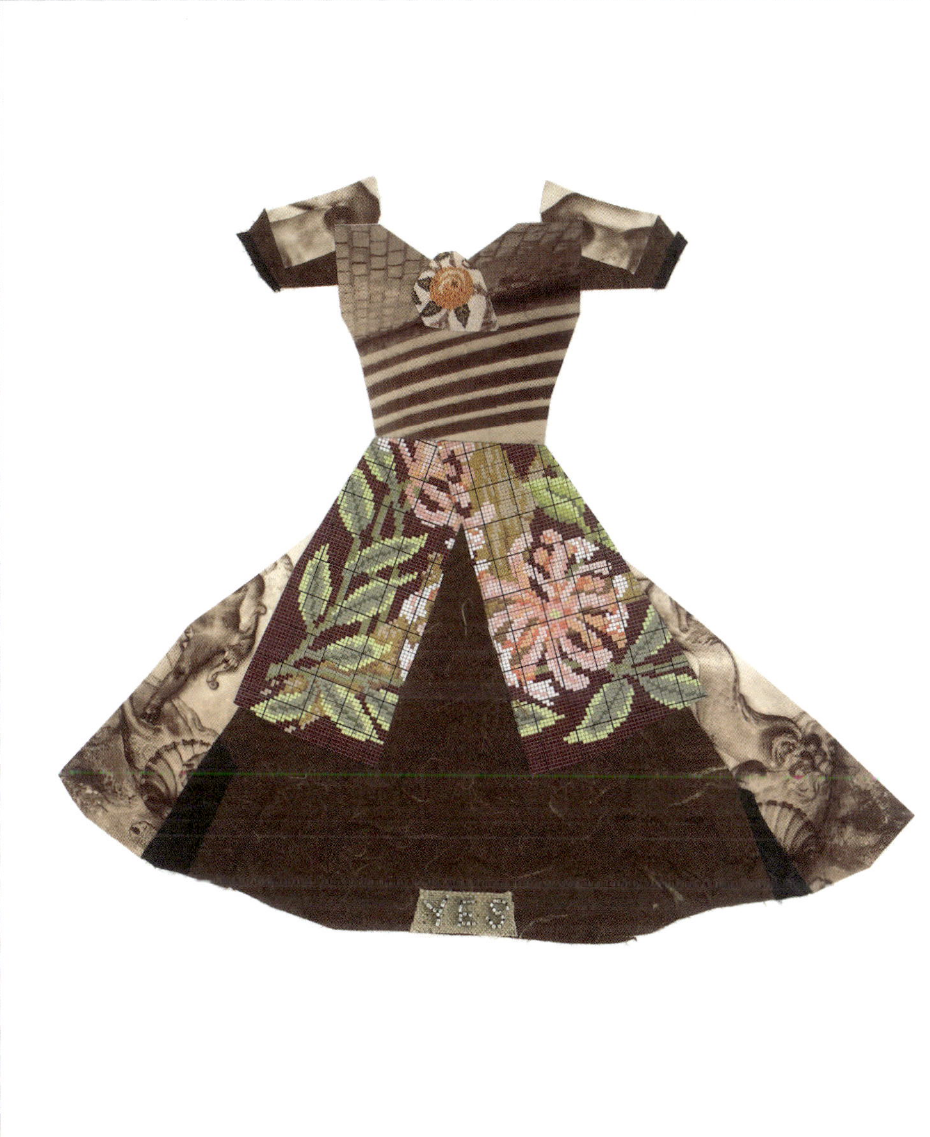
YES

MANASSAS

1917

10,000 Negroes parade down Fifth Avenue in New York City
in protest against lynchings in the South.
The marchers include NAACP leaders W.E.B. DuBois
and James Weldon Johnson.

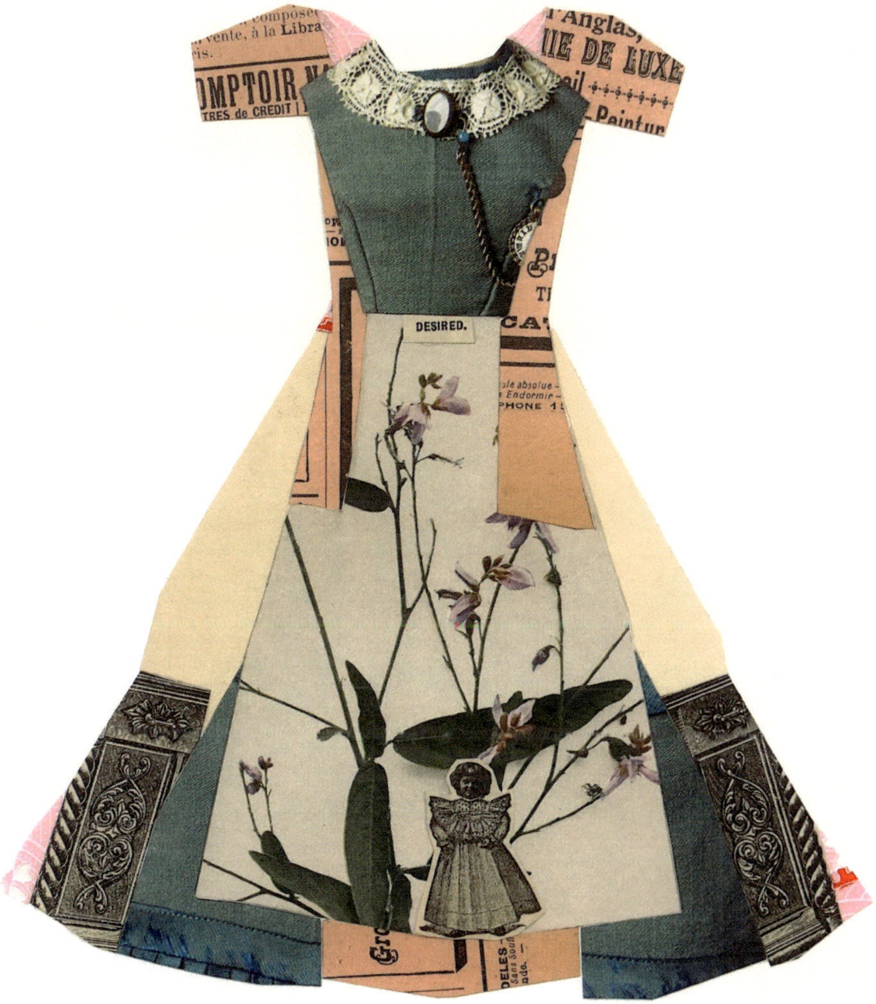
DESIRED.

PALATKA

1935

Founding by Mary McLeod Bethune of the National Council of Negro Women.

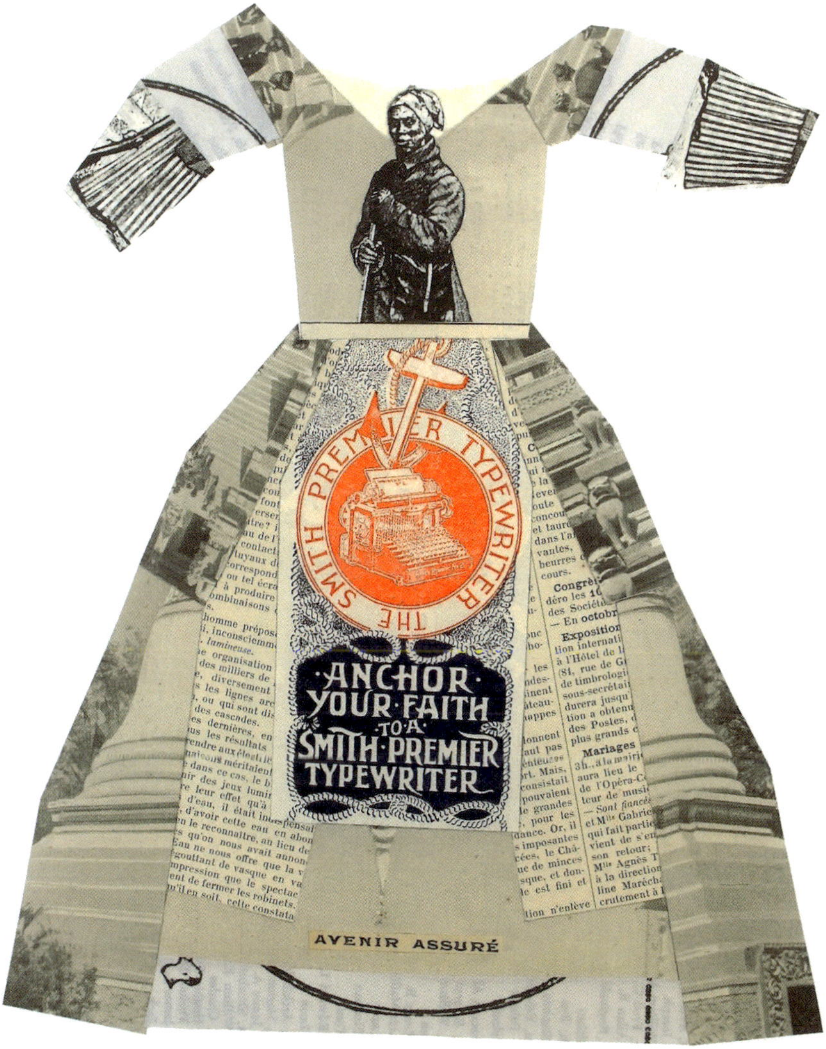
THE SMITH PREMIER TYPEWRITER
ANCHOR YOUR FAITH TO A SMITH PREMIER TYPEWRITER
AVENIR ASSURÉ

DOWAGIAC

1939

Marian Anderson, denied the use of Constitution Hall
by the Daughters of The American Revolution,
sings on Easter Sunday before 75,000 people
assembled on the National Mall in
Washington, D.C.

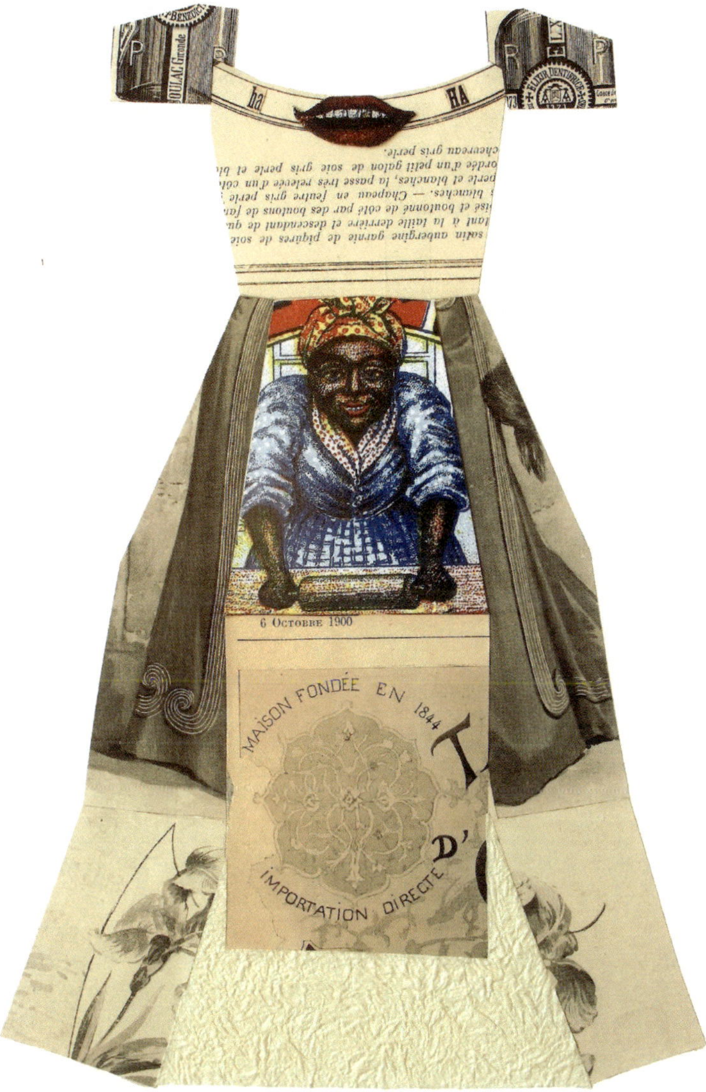
ha
HA
6 Octobre 1900
MAISON FONDÉE EN 1844
IMPORTATION DIRECTE

MINOT

1939

Jane Bolin is appointed judge of the Court of Domestic Relations in New York City—thus becoming the first Negro woman judge in the United States.

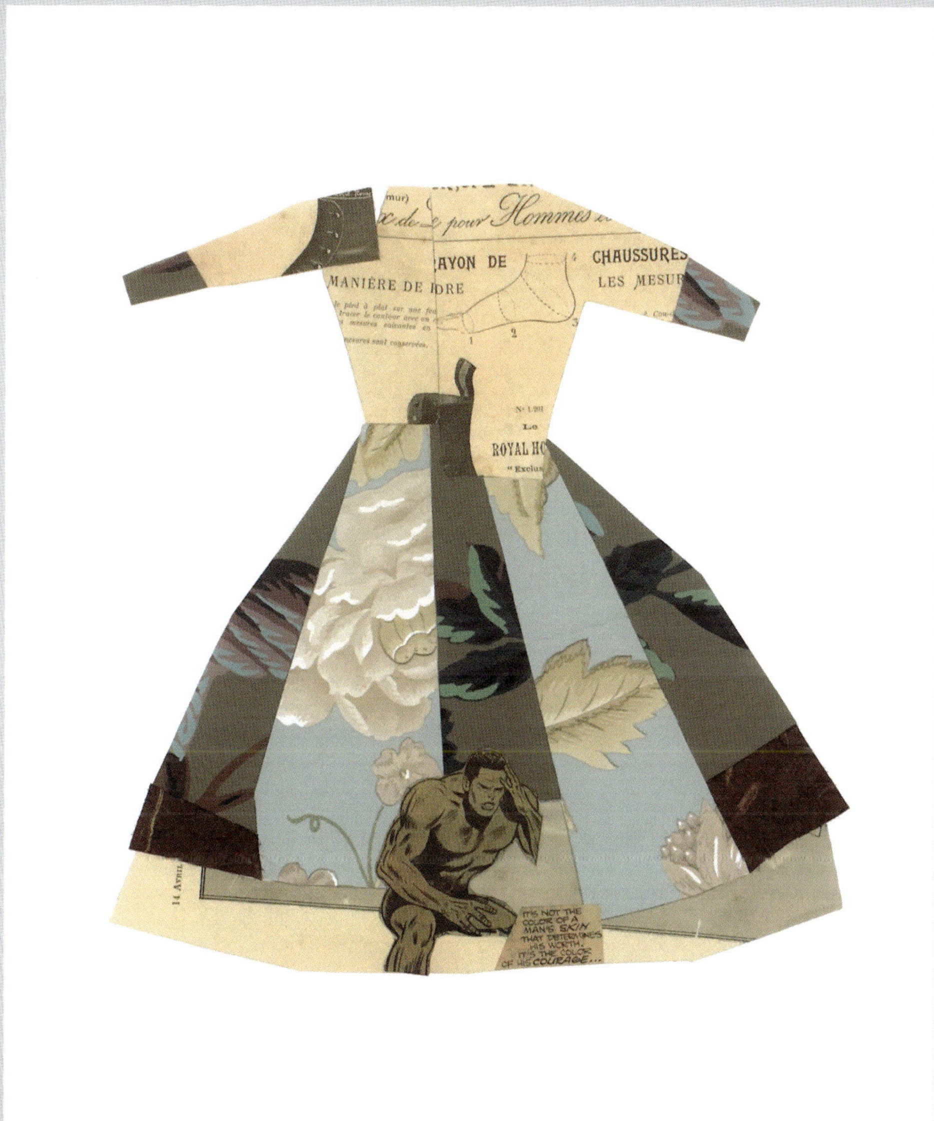
pour Hommes
RAYON DE
CHAUSSURES
MANIÈRE DE
LES MESUR
ROYAL HO
IT'S NOT THE COLOR OF A MAN'S SKIN THAT DETERMINES HIS WORTH. IT'S THE COLOR OF HIS COURAGE...

ELIZABETHTOWN

1941

The Supreme Court—in a case brought by Congressman Arthur Mitchell—rules that separate facilities in railroad travel must be substantially equal.

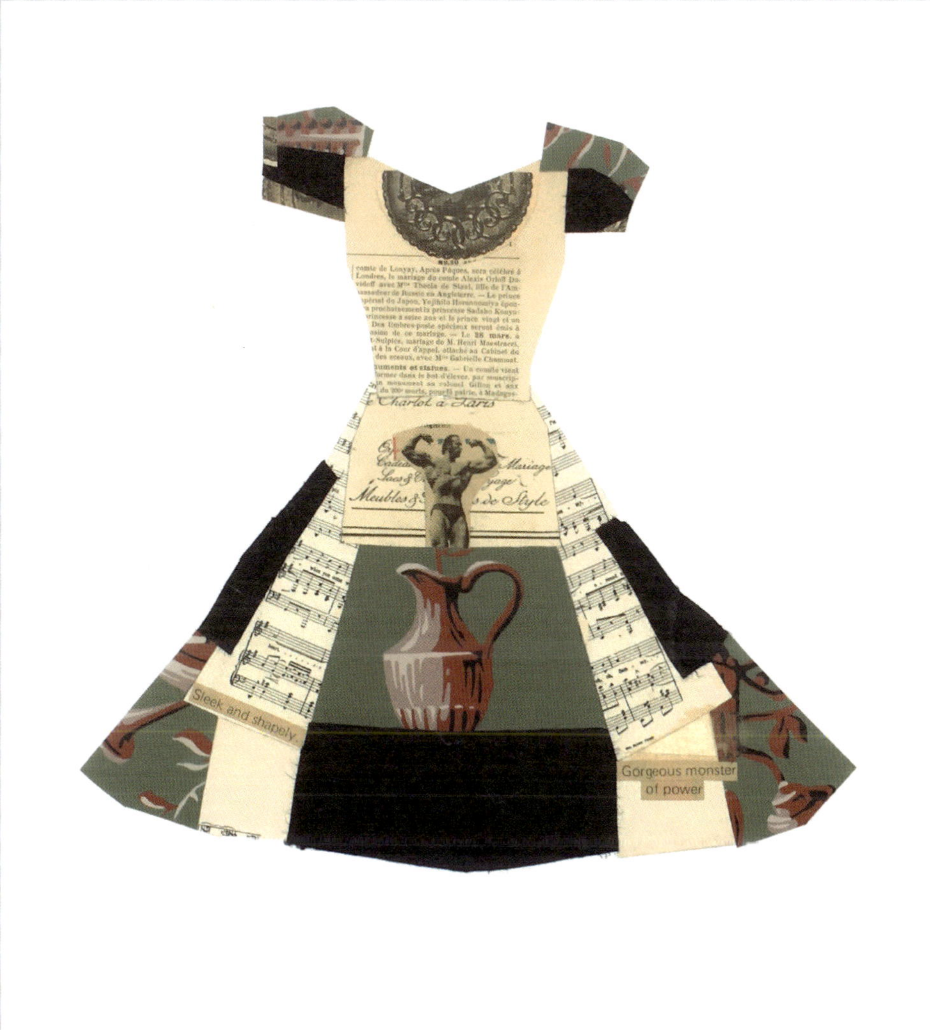
Charlot à Paris
Mariage
Meubles &
de Style
Sleek and shapely.
Gorgeous monster of power

DEL RIO

1947

The Truman committee on civil rights formally condemns racial injustice in America in the widely quoted report "To Secure These Rights."

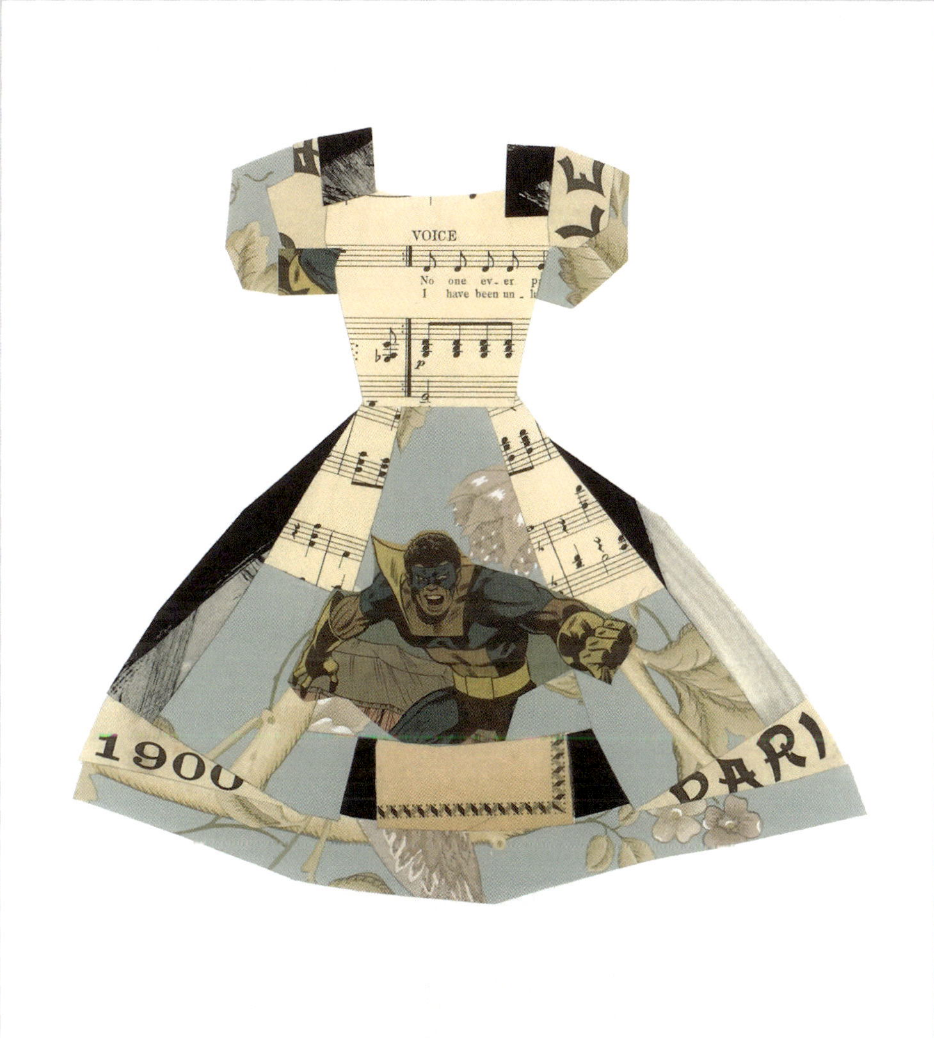
VOICE
No one ev-er p
I have been un-l
1900
PARI

JESUP

1950

Ralph Bunche wins the Nobel Peace Prize.

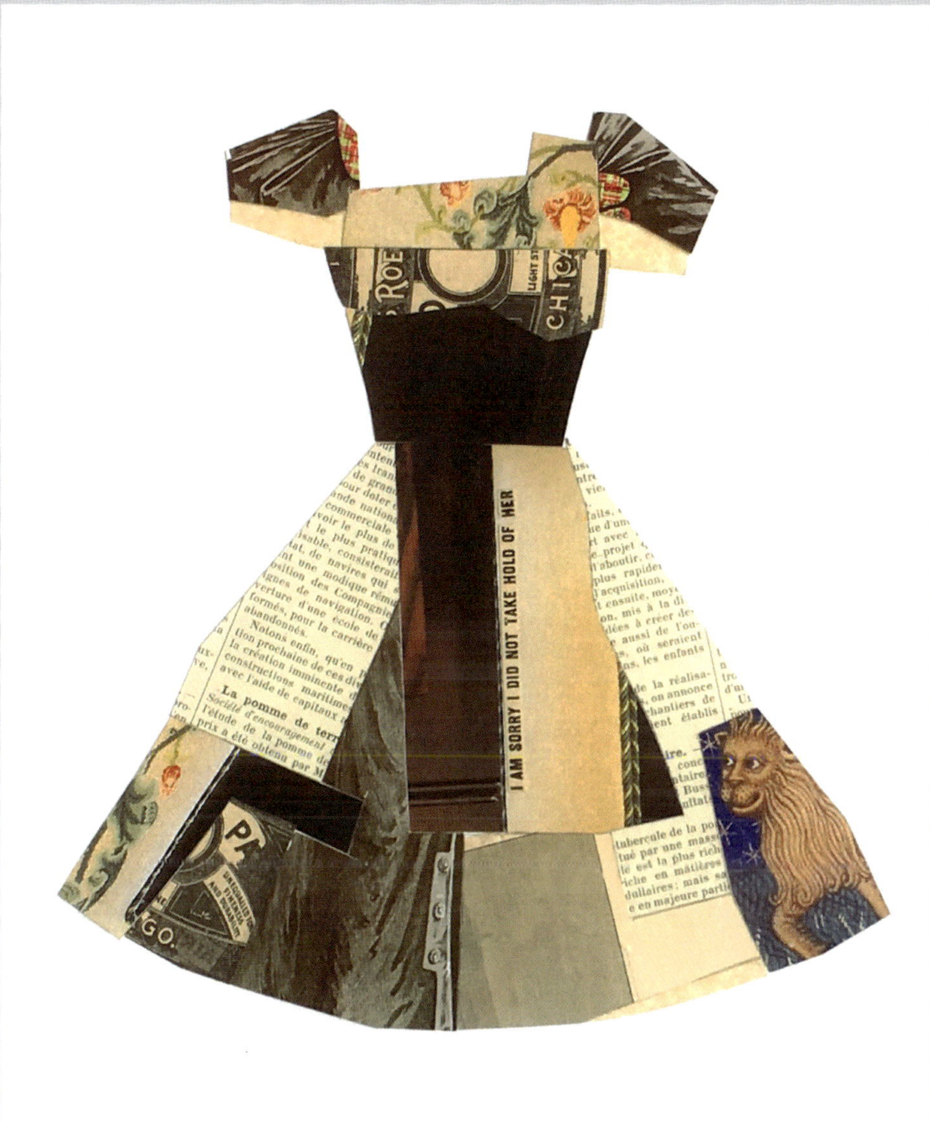
I AM SORRY I DID NOT TAKE HOLD OF HER

GASTONIA

1950

Gwendolyn Brooks is awarded a Pulitzer Prize for poetry.

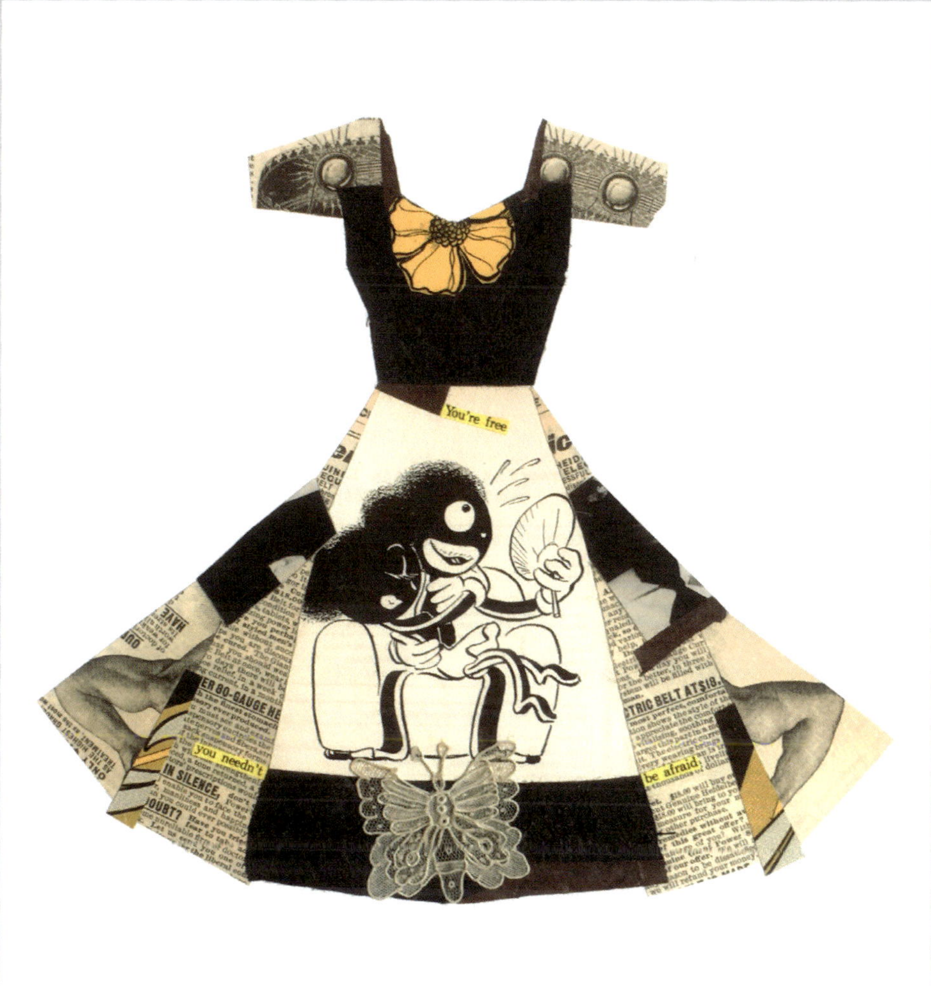
You're free
you needn't
be afraid.
IN SILENCE,

LOVE IS THE ONLY THING

I love, and you love
We love, sweet love
I look and you look
And we found sweet love
And now we know

Love is the only thing that matters at all
After all

I kiss, and you kiss
Each kiss, sweet lips
I tease and you squeeze
And we find sweet bliss
That's how we know

Love is the only thing that matters at all
After all

I'm lucky
And you're lucky, too
We're lucky
And we know it's true
Love is so wonderful

I give, and you give
We live, for love
Each night, each day
We love sweet love
'Cause ain't it so?

Love is the only thing that matters at all
After all

Love is the only thing that matters at all
After all

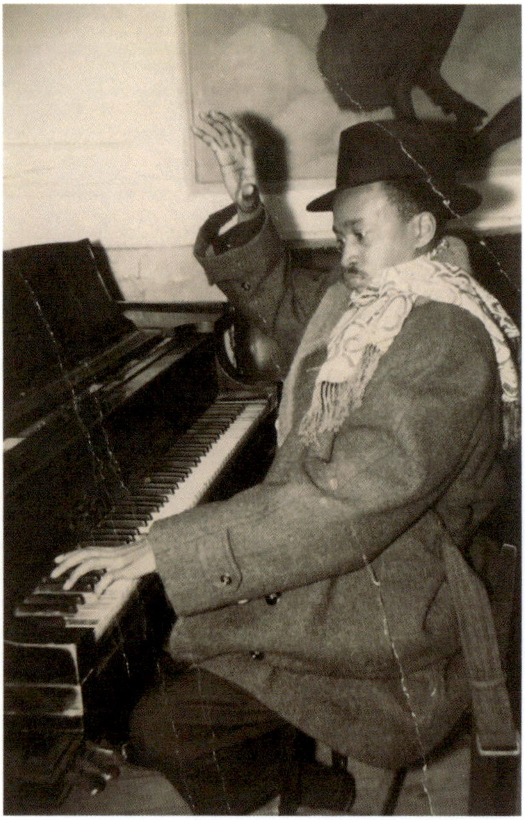

NOTES

Lyrics in the section Whistles & Stops were written by the author's father, John L. McFarland. McFarland wrote *Won't Be Long* and *Love is the Only Thing* for Aretha Franklin, who sang them on her early albums for Columbia Records.

Facts cited in the section Whistles & Stops appear in *The Negro Almanac of 1972* published by the Bellwether Company.

Background text in Pathfinder comes from *Incidents in the Life of a Slave Girl*, by Harriet Jacobs, first published in 1861.

SPECIAL THANKS TO:

Mia Brandt, Marsha Grant, Katherine Leiner, Gretta Keene, and Anne Adams for their constancy, love, and support.

Gloria and Lorna McFarland, Stephen and Lissie Thomas, Dillon Dyer, and Gail Benjamin for their enduring love.

Kevin Thomas, in memoriam, for his moral guidance and unshakeable faith in the life of the mind.

Editors Elizabeth Murphy of Grid Books and Nancy White of The Word Works for their enthusiasm for this work.

Designers Michael Russem and Diane Bertolo for their aesthetic expertise.

The thousands of Pullman Porters who perfected the art of railroad travel in the United States from 1867–1969.

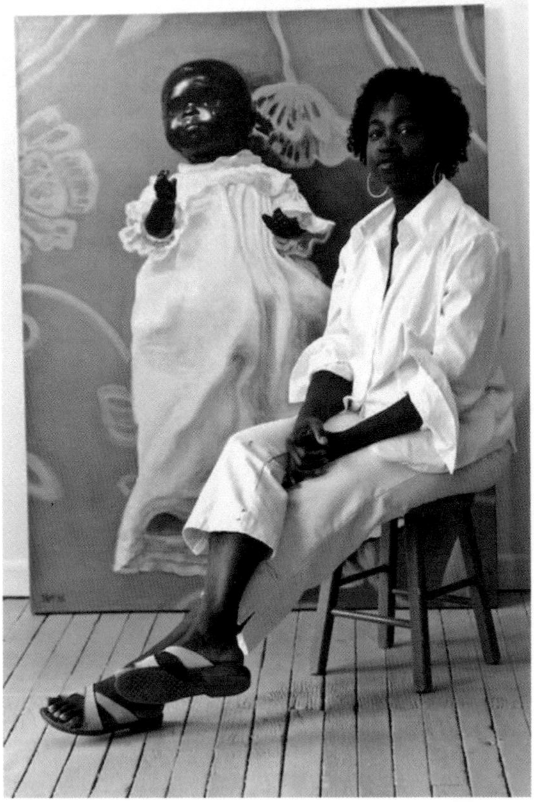

PHOTO BY RACHEL ELIZA GRIFFITHS

JoAnne McFarland is an artist, poet, and curator and the Artistic Director of Artpoetica Project Space in Gowanus, Brooklyn which exhibits experimental and hybrid works that focus on the intersection of language and visual representation. JoAnne is the former Exhibitions Director of A.I.R. Gallery. She has artwork in the permanent collections of The Library of Congress, The Columbus Museum of Art, and The Department of State, among many others. JoAnne's poetry collections include: *Tracks of My Tears, Said I Meant* (a collaboration with poet Paul Eprile), *Identifying the Body, Fossil Fuel, 13 Ways of Looking at a Black Girl,* and *Acid Rain*. Her curatorial project Sally, a collaboration with artist Sasha Chavchavadze that began in 2019, focuses on women, like Sally Hemings, whose lives have been marginalized, or forgotten. Sally has traveled to nine national venues, featuring the work of fifty artists. JoAnne has had fellowships at The Painting Center, The Bard Graduate Center Library, KALA Art Institute, The National Arts Club, The Van Alen Institute, and Cave Canem. JoAnne's recent shows include *Queen For a Day* at the Bard Graduate Center Library, *Rights & Wrongs* at The Carroll Mansion in Baltimore, MD, and *Best & Brightest* and *The Indivisible Spectrum*, both at The Painting Center in NYC.